BROADCAST RIGHTS

The Future of TV and Streaming

By Luke Hanlon

An Imprint of Abdo Publishing
abdobooks.com

abdobooks.com

Printed in the United States of America, North Mankato, Minnesota.
102025
012026

Cover Photo: Ric Tapia/Getty Images Sport/Getty Images
Interior Photos: Thomas B. Shea/Getty Images Sport/Getty Images, 1, 12; Ira L. Black/Corbis/Getty Images Sport/Getty Images, 3, 39; Paul Tepley Collection/Diamond Images/Getty Images, 4–5; Perry Knotts/Getty Images Sport/Getty Images, 6–7; C. Morgan Engel/NCAA Photos/Getty Images, 8–9, 45; Dylan Buell/Getty Images Sport/Getty Images, 10–11; Michael Owens/Getty Images Sport/Getty Images, 15; Alejandra Villa Loarca/Newsday RM/Newsday LLC/Getty Images, 16, 47; Jari Pestelacci/Eurasia Sport Images/Getty Images Sport/Getty Images, 17; Todd Kirkland/Getty Images Sport/Getty Images, 19; K. C. Alfred/ZUMA Press, Inc./Alamy, 20; Jim McIsaac/Getty Images Sport/Getty Images, 22–23; Askar Karimullin/Alamy, 25; HO/AFP/Getty Images, 26–27; Focus On Sport/Getty Images Sport/Getty Images, 28; Robin Alam/Icon Sportswire/Getty Images, 30–31; Augusta National/Masters Historic Imagery/Getty Images, 32–33; Maddie Meyer/Getty Images Sport/Getty Images, 34–35; David Rosenblum/Icon Sportswire/Getty Images, 36; Michael Hickey/Getty Images Sport/Getty Images, 37; Harry How/Getty Images Sport/Getty Images, 41; Emilee Chinn/Getty Images Sport/Getty Images, 42–43

Editor: Christa Kelly
Series Designer: Maggie Villaume

Library of Congress Control Number: 2025939176

Publisher's Cataloging-in-Publication Data

Names: Hanlon, Luke, author.
Title: Broadcast rights: the future of tv and streaming / by Luke Hanlon
Description: Minneapolis, Minnesota: Abdo Publishing, 2026 | Series: The business of sports | Includes online resources and index.
Identifiers: ISBN 9781098298241 (lib. bdg.) | ISBN 9798384932048 (ebook)
Subjects: LCSH: Sports--Juvenile literature. | Sports journalism--Juvenile literature. | Sports broadcasting--Juvenile literature. | Mass media and sports--Juvenile literature. | Sportscasters--Juvenile literature. | Sports in popular culture--Juvenile literature.
Classification: DDC 070.449796--dc23

TABLE OF CONTENTS

52

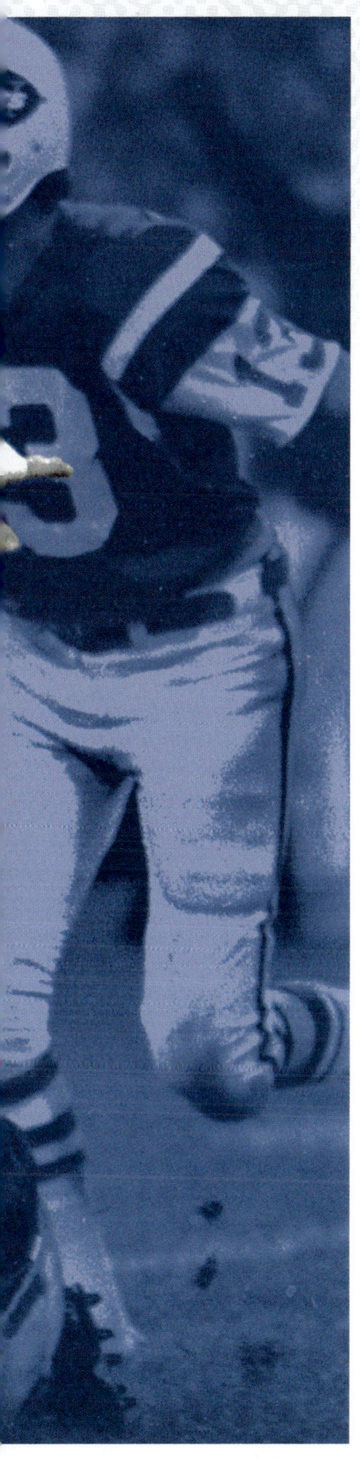

CHAPTER ONE

A TV INSTITUTION

For 50 years, the National Football League (NFL) broadcast its games only on Sundays. In 1970, the league decided to add one game a week on Monday nights. But it needed a network to air the games.

The TV network ABC saw big potential in airing the games. With just one game on and a national audience, the network thought a lot of people would watch the broadcast. ABC could then charge companies to place commercials in the broadcast. ABC paid $8.5 million to buy the rights to air the games. The network aired the first Monday night game on September 21, 1970. Viewers watched the New York Jets take on the Cleveland Browns. With that, *Monday Night Football* was born.

The New York Jets beat the Cleveland Browns 31–21 on the first broadcast of *Monday Night Football.*

Broadcasting the game turned out to be a huge success for both the NFL and ABC. More than one million people in New York alone watched the first *Monday Night Football* broadcast. Viewers quickly changed their habits to make sure they were home on Monday nights to watch football.

For 36 years, NFL fans tuned in to ABC to watch *Monday Night Football*. The broadcast often attracted high ratings. That helped ABC bring in a lot of ad revenue. But the NFL kept raising its broadcasting fee. The games eventually became too expensive for the network. By 2005, ABC was paying $550 million a year to air the games. Even with ads, the company was losing $150 million each year on *Monday Night Football*.

Before the 2006 NFL season, ESPN paid $1.1 billion for the broadcasting rights to *Monday Night Football*. The move helped increase ESPN's ratings. Each NFL game attracted millions of viewers. So the cable channel kept paying more to extend the deal. In 2021, ESPN agreed to pay the NFL

Joe Buck, *left*, and Troy Aikman, *right*, began announcing NFL games together in 2002. In 2022, the pair started calling *Monday Night Football*.

ESPN AND ABC

ESPN started as a small sports cable channel in 1978. Six years later, ABC bought ESPN for $188 million. The move helped ABC expand its sports coverage. In 1996, the Walt Disney Company bought ABC. It also gained control of ESPN. During football season, the two channels will often show the same games. Airing the games on both channels boosts the games' overall ratings. This practice is called simulcasting. ABC and ESPN simulcast 14 games together during the 2024 NFL season. The two channels will each air the Super Bowl following the 2026 and 2030 seasons.

$2.7 billion a year to keep *Monday Night Football* until 2033.

Before long, ESPN was trusted with the biggest game of the year. In March 2022, ESPN announced that it would be airing the Super Bowl following the 2026 season and the 2030 season. The network had never broadcast a Super Bowl before. The network had made it big.

TV Gold

The landscape of live TV has changed over the years. During TV's rise in popularity in the 1960s, American viewers could choose between only three channels. Today, viewers have nearly unlimited options of shows to watch. Some cable and satellite TV packages feature hundreds of channels. And streaming services offer the ability to watch shows and movies on demand. The abundance of viewing options has caused a sharp decline in ratings for TV shows since the mid-2010s. Shows have to try harder to attract audiences.

Today, people can watch more than a dozen sports on demand.

Though people have more entertainment options than ever before, live sports continue to draw large audiences. This helps sports ratings continue to thrive. As such, buying rights for live sports remains a top priority for networks and streaming services alike.

Wilson
Lilly
ACES
51

CHAPTER TWO

THE VALUE OF BROADCASTING

Televising live sporting events is a key factor in the success of any sports league. Making it easy for viewers to watch games helps keep fans engaged with the league. Many leagues broadcast games around the world to attract as many fans as possible.

Leagues also have financial reasons for selling broadcasting rights. Leagues around the world make billions of dollars each year from TV deals. Some leagues make the majority of their money by selling broadcasting rights. For example, the NFL made $23 billion in 2024. More than $12 billion came from the league's deals with its broadcasting partners.

Eighty-five percent of US sports fans prefer watching sports on TV over watching events in person.

In 2025, the NFL had broadcasting deals with nearly a dozen companies, including CBS, FOX, ESPN, Peacock, and Netflix.

Making Money

It's expensive to buy the broadcasting rights for big leagues. But networks can make their money back through cable subscriptions and ad revenue. Companies pay networks to run commercials during their broadcasts. The price of a 30-second commercial varies based on an event's ratings. The more viewers a show regularly gets, the more money networks can charge for ads.

More than 20 million people watch *Sunday Night Football* each week on NBC. In 2023, the network charged an average of $882,079 for a 30-second ad. Meanwhile, NBC's singing competition series *The Voice* attracts about 5 million viewers per episode. Advertisers paid an average of $125,833 to air a commercial during the show.

For decades, networks have used TV ratings to decide how much to charge to air ads. In 1950, Nielsen Media Research began recording what Americans watch on TV. Nielsen randomly chooses households around the country. The company connects devices to the households' TVs. The devices record what people in the household are watching. By 2022, Nielsen had devices in about 42,000 US homes. The company then uses the data it collects to estimate a show's total number of viewers.

BIG MONEY FOR THE BIG GAME

The Super Bowl is the most watched TV event every year. More than 100 million people tune in annually. There is no broadcast that attracts more demand from advertisers. Super Bowl commercials have become as much a part of American culture as the game itself. Airing a commercial during the Super Bowl often costs companies millions of dollars. In 2024, it cost $7 million for a 30-second ad.

Knowing who is watching a certain program is just as important to advertisers as how many people are watching it. Nielsen tracks a lot of data about the people who use its recording devices. The company knows the ages of the people it tracks. Nielsen breaks down its ratings into age demographics. Advertisers often want to reach young people the most. That's because advertisers believe they can influence young people more than older people. So sports leagues often try to attract young people to watch their games.

All Kinds of Deals

National broadcasting rights account for the biggest sports TV deals. Typically only a small number of a league's games are shown to a national audience each season. But those games capture the most viewers.

Many American sports leagues also rely on smaller regional sports deals. The NBA, the Women's National Basketball Association (WNBA), the National Hockey League (NHL), and Major League Baseball (MLB) are just a few of the leagues that have deals with regional sports networks (RSNs). These channels allow fans to watch their favorite local teams.

RSNs broadcast live games within a certain area. For example, local channels in the state of Washington air Seattle Storm WNBA games that aren't broadcast nationally. This lets fans cheer on their favorite teams even when their games aren't widely broadcast.

Regional TV deals are particularly important for MLB. Each MLB team plays 162 games in a season. A handful of those games are broadcast nationally. The rest are available on RSNs.

In 2024, Nielsen Media Research found that Americans watched 519.4 billion minutes of NFL games.

In 2023, an average of 2.3 million viewers tuned in to RSNs each day to watch their local MLB teams.

MLB has smaller national media deals than the NFL and NBA. This means MLB relies on regional deals to make money. About 25 percent of the league's revenue is made through

Baseball is the second-most popular sport to watch in the United States.

deals with RSNs. That is higher than any other American sports league.

TV networks value the consistent programming that sports offer. At the same time, some events are valuable because they're rarer. For example, the Olympic Games and FIFA World

In 2024, people spent 28.7 billion hours watching TV coverage of the Olympic Games in Paris, France.

Cups take place only every four years. The novelty of these events helps them draw massive audiences. Networks hope that these broadcasts will increase their ratings more broadly.

An estimated 1.5 billion people around the globe watched soccer icon Lionel Messi and Argentina defeat France in the 2022 men's World Cup final. A record audience of 16.7 million of those viewers were from the United States. That helped the FOX TV channel justify the $425 million it paid to broadcast every men's and women's World Cup from 2015 to 2022.

Adapting to Change

The way fans watch live games is much different now than in the past. As more people got rid of cable and satellite packages, Nielsen's tracking system began to feel outdated. The company's system didn't account for streaming services.

The tension between networks and Nielsen came to a head in 2020 during the COVID-19 pandemic. During that time, Nielsen couldn't send employees to homes to check their equipment. This led to inaccurate ratings. The flawed ratings made many networks lose ad revenue.

Nielsen began tracking ratings more accurately in September 2020. That's when the company began counting out-of-home viewers of nationally broadcast events. Those being monitored by Nielsen could use a device to count how many household members were watching TV away from their homes. No programs saw bigger increases in ratings than sporting events. That's because fans regularly gather to watch games together.

TV ratings continue to be the main factor in determining the the ad revenue networks make. Ratings also still determine the price networks pay for broadcasting rights. In 2024, 94 out of the 100 most watched programs in the United States were NFL games. It's no surprise then that the NFL makes

In 2024, NBC charged more than $1 million for a 30-second ad on *Sunday Night Football.*

more from broadcasting deals than any other US sports league. But even sporting events with modest TV ratings can still be worth billions.

In 2024, the NBA needed to sign new national broadcasting deals. Viewership had sharply declined during the pandemic, which had disrupted the league's schedule. Ratings increased once the league returned to its normal schedule. But they were still much lower than ratings for the 2018–19 season.

The declining ratings didn't seem to bother the networks bidding for the NBA's broadcasting rights. Amazon, ESPN, and NBC signed massive 11-year deals with the NBA and the WNBA. The companies will pay $77 billion for broadcasting rights to the NBA and the WNBA. ESPN alone is paying the leagues a combined $2.62 billion per year. This is only slightly less than the $2.7 billion it pays to air NFL games.

NBA games have far lower ratings than NFL games. But networks still see the NBA as extremely valuable. This is partially because the NBA plays so many games. Each NBA team plays an 82-game season. NFL teams play only 17 games per season. And though the NBA's ratings are down, they are still higher than the ratings for most programs. This combination of factors makes the league's broadcasting rights valuable.

FOX hosts a pregame show called *FOX NFL Sunday* before each Sunday's NFL games.

CASE STUDY

FOX CHANGES THE GAME

The TV network CBS began broadcasting NFL games in 1956. When the NFL shopped for new broadcasting deals in 1993, the league assumed CBS would continue to be one of its partners. However, FOX bid $1.6 billion for the right to air NFL games. The NFL went with FOX's offer, ending its long relationship with CBS.

FOX wanted to broadcast games differently than networks had in the past. The network added a permanent scorebox onto the screen. That way, fans always knew the score of the game. FOX also wanted its broadcasts to be fun. The network told its analysts to put less focus on strategy during pregame shows. Instead, FOX encouraged them to tell jokes. FOX told the commentators not to take games too seriously.

The new graphics and relaxed pregame shows were hits right away. The NFL's ratings helped FOX gain credibility. By 2024, FOX had aired nearly a dozen Super Bowls, more than any other network.

Meanwhile, CBS saw a massive decline in its ratings. Four years after losing the contract, CBS had a chance to buy NFL rights again. This time, CBS spent $4 billion over eight years to bring the NFL back to its airwaves.

CHAPTER THREE

STREAMING TAKEOVER

On August 26, 2002, New York Yankees second baseman Alfonso Soriano blasted his 31st home run of the season. His homer helped the Yankees earn a 10–3 win against the Texas Rangers. And it made him the first second baseman to ever hit more than 30 home runs in a season for the Yankees.

Soriano's achievement wasn't the most significant milestone of the day, though. For years, only fans in Texas or New York would have been able to watch the record-breaking game. But more than 30,000 baseball fans from around the world watched the game that day. MLB.TV live streamed it online. MLB became the first major sports league to broadcast a live game on the internet.

MLB.TV displayed the Yankees–Rangers game on a tiny box. The video quality was blurry. But it

Alfonso Soriano played for the New York Yankees from 1999 to 2003, then again in 2013 and 2014.

proved to be a monumental broadcast for sports fans. More than two decades later, nearly half of all TV is streamed. This new technology has led to massive growth in the number of sporting events that are live streamed.

ESPN+

ESPN first aired a live sporting event in 1979. Since then, the channel has been dedicated to sports programming. In 2018, the channel expanded its sports coverage even further by launching a streaming service called ESPN+.

ESPN+ offered a platform for viewers to watch additional sporting events. And unlike with ESPN's traditional channels, subscribers to the streaming service could choose what they wanted to watch. In 2025, ESPN+ subscribers had access to more than 27,000 hours of live sports. That included expanded coverage of professional leagues such as the NHL and MLB. ESPN+ also provided access to thousands of college sporting events. Fans could watch these games anywhere they had internet access.

Following the success of ESPN+, more networks began to expand their streaming coverage of sports. In July 2020, NBC's owner, Comcast, launched Peacock. Less than a year later, CBS debuted Paramount+. These services primarily focused on TV shows and movies. But they also expanded access to

ESPN is headquartered in Bristol, Connecticut.

ESPN

live sports. Since both networks had NFL broadcasting rights, fans could stream live games. The streaming services also offered coverage of international soccer leagues, college sports, golf tournaments, and more. The increased streaming competition provided sports fans with the opportunity to watch more games than ever before.

Streaming the Olympics

In 1936, people gathered in public auditoriums around Germany. The Olympic Games were taking place in Berlin, the nation's capital. And for the first time, fans could follow events from the Olympics live on a screen. Viewers gained even more access when Rome, Italy, hosted the Summer Games in 1960. That year, networks broadcast the Olympics internationally.

For decades, fans have gathered around their TVs to watch the world's best athletes compete at the Olympics. But for much of that time, fans could only watch what the networks provided. Many events were never shown on TV. And some of the events shown on TV were not live.

In 1980, the US men's hockey team faced off against the Soviet Union during the 1980 Winter Olympics in Lake Placid, New York. The United States won in a stunning turn of events that came to be known as "The Miracle on Ice." But viewers

In 1936, more than 162,000 people in Germany watched the Olympic Games on TV.

in the United States were not able to watch the game live. Instead, the game aired on TV three hours later. The networks preferred to show events in prime time to get better ratings.

The internet changed the way the Olympic Games were broadcast. With each passing Olympics, live coverage continued to expand. In the United States, NBC has broadcast

The US men's hockey team beat the Soviet Union 4–3 during the 1980 Winter Olympics, delivering an incredible upset.

each Summer Games since 1988. One of the reasons the network launched Peacock in July 2020 was to have it ready to live stream events at the 2020 Olympics in Tokyo, Japan. However, the pandemic delayed the Olympic Games to the summer of 2021. Even with the additional time to prepare, Peacock didn't offer live coverage of every event. And the app often experienced technical difficulties during broadcasts.

Peacock changed its strategy ahead of the 2024 Summer Games in Paris, France. That year, the app live streamed every event at the Olympics and Paralympics. Viewers streamed more than 17 billion minutes of live coverage on Peacock. That surpassed the streaming viewership of all previous Summer and Winter Olympics combined.

Tech Disruptors

Big technology companies such as Amazon, Apple, and Google make tens of billions in revenue each year. With plenty of money to spend, each of these companies has launched its own streaming platform. They use their streaming services to create original shows and movies. But each company has also dipped into live sports in an effort to increase their number of subscribers.

Amazon was the first of the companies to make a big move into sports broadcasting rights. Before the 2017 NFL season, Amazon paid the league $50 million a year to stream 10 *Thursday Night Football* games on its streaming service, Prime Video. The games were simultaneously broadcast on TV. However, in 2021, Amazon wanted exclusive rights for *Thursday Night Football*. The company paid the NFL $1 billion per year to keep Thursday night games on Prime Video from 2023 to 2033. In the NFL, games are always shown on free over-the-air

JOHNSON
30

channels in their local markets. But now anyone else who wants to watch Thursday Night Football must have Prime Video.

Amazon quickly saw the benefits of the deal. Viewership for *Thursday Night Football* increased in 2024. And Prime Video gained subscribers. After its success in broadcasting NFL games, Amazon bought broadcasting rights for the NBA, the WNBA, NASCAR, and more.

Many tech companies have bought broadcasting rights to a few select games. Apple TV+ started with that strategy as well. In 2022, the streaming service began airing MLB games on Friday nights.

Apple expanded its sports coverage dramatically in 2023. That year, the company paid $2.5 billion to have rights to Major League Soccer (MLS) for 10 years. MLS became the first American sports league to have all its games broadcast on a streaming service.

Moving away from traditional TV channels was a risk for MLS. The league could have lost fans. Some games were still broadcast nationally. But many of the league's games were accessible only by subscribing to the MLS Season Pass on Apple TV+.

Many are watching to see how the deal plays out. There have been some positives so far. When Lionel Messi joined Inter Miami FC in 2023, the number of Apple TV+ subscribers soared.

In 2024, *Thursday Night Football* attracted an average of 13.2 million viewers.

STREAMING SPORTS ON NETFLIX

Netflix was founded in 1998. It began as a business that allowed people to rent DVDs through the mail. In 2007, the company launched its streaming service. More than 15 years later, the service began airing live sporting events. Its biggest event came in 2024. In November, legendary boxer Mike Tyson fought YouTube star Jake Paul in a boxing match. More than 108 million people around the world watched the fight. That made it the most streamed sporting event ever.

Before the superstar came to MLS, a majority of the league's streaming service subscribers were based in the United States. After Messi's move, Apple TV+ saw a big boost in subscribers from around the world. However, others have noted that the deal limits MLS's visibility. When the 2024 MLS Cup saw a major decline in TV ratings, many wondered if the league was missing out on casual fans.

CASE STUDY

A BROADCAST UNLIKE ANY OTHER

Every April, Augusta National Golf Club in Georgia hosts the Masters. Billed as "a tradition unlike any other," the Masters is unique. CBS's relationship with the Masters is also unlike any other broadcasting rights deal. In 2025, CBS aired the tournament for the 70th straight year. That's the longest-running relationship between a network and a sporting event.

The terms of the partnership between the tournament and the network are different from any other TV deal. The Masters doesn't charge CBS for broadcasting rights. For an event that regularly gets more than 10 million viewers, experts project the Masters could charge $125 million for broadcasting rights. But by not charging CBS, the Masters has more control over the broadcast.

The Masters makes sure broadcasters call people who watch the tournament in person "patrons," not fans. Broadcasters aren't allowed to mention how much money the winning players make. CBS also doesn't profit as much from the Masters as it could. That's because the network airs significantly fewer commercials during the Masters than are usually aired during sporting events.

The Masters has been broadcast since 1956.

BIG EAST
CONN
HUSKIES
Wilson

CHAPTER FOUR

CHANGING THE GAME

Broadcasting rights influence every aspect of modern sports. The money paid by networks to leagues affects much more than just those two parties. Teams, players, and fans are all impacted by the decisions made by TV executives and the heads of leagues.

The money to be made from TV deals has led to huge changes to college sports since the 2010s. College sports make most of their money by selling broadcasting rights. TV deals can encourage teams to join conferences. They can also doom conferences.

The Big Ten Conference signed a seven-year deal for $7 billion. The Southeastern Conference signed a 10-year deal for $3 billion. These conferences have become extremely popular. Their games are broadcast

In 2024, ESPN's women's college basketball games had an average viewership of 280,000 people.

In 2025, the Big Ten Conference had broadcasting deals with CBS, FOX, Peacock, and more.

around the country. This draws both longtime fans and new fans.

Other conferences haven't been as successful. In 1915, the Pacific Coast Conference, also known as the Pac-12, was founded. The University of California, the University of Oregon, Oregon State, and the University of Washington played in the conference for more than 100 years. By the 2020s, the Pac-12 boasted successful athletic programs such as the University of California, Los Angeles (UCLA), the University of Southern California (USC), and Stanford University.

During the 2023–2024 season, the Pac-12 struggled to sign a new TV deal. Without a broadcasting deal, the conference's future seemed unstable. Ten of the 12 teams in the conference left.

Oregon, UCLA, USC, and Washington moved to the Big Ten Conference. That conference is mainly based in the Midwest. California and Stanford moved to the Atlantic Coast Conference. This conference is based on the East Coast. Even though the decision was made mostly due to the schools' football teams, it had far-reaching impacts. Every team at these schools had to change conferences.

The University of Oregon's football team won the Big Ten championship in 2024, the team's first year in the conference.

THE CAITLIN CLARK EFFECT

Players are often affected by TV deals. But some players can also affect how much TV deals are worth. During her final two seasons playing for the University of Iowa's women's basketball team, Caitlin Clark helped set multiple viewership records for women's basketball. In her rookie WNBA season in 2024, the league experienced a massive increase in TV ratings. During that season, the league agreed to a new media deal worth $200 million a year. The WNBA's old deal made just $50 million a year.

Affecting the Fans

The constantly changing world of sports broadcasting has transformed how sports fans watch games. Today, fans have far more access to live sports than ever before. But watching those games comes with a price.

When MLS played its first season in 1996, it was the only soccer league in the world that Americans could watch on TV. In 2011, FOX began broadcasting live English Premier League games in the United States. The top leagues in countries such as Germany, Italy, Spain, and France eventually sold broadcasting rights to US partners as well. By the 2020s, an American soccer fan could watch any MLS or National Women's Soccer League game while also following their favorite international teams.

Finding all of those live broadcasts can be a challenge for fans. A Premier League fan from the United States can watch games on NBC. But the league also airs some games only on the streaming service Peacock. And teams in England play

National Women's Soccer League games are broadcast on 12 different TV networks and streaming services.

in multiple tournaments. To watch the Football Association Challenge Cup, fans need ESPN+. If a fan's favorite Premier League team makes the Champions League, they need Paramount+ to watch those games. And an MLS fan needs Apple TV+ to watch their local team.

NFL games have traditionally been easy for fans to follow. Most NFL games air on CBS, FOX, and NBC. But some games cost extra to watch. To watch games on Mondays, a fan needs a cable package that includes ESPN. Then they need a Prime Video subscription to watch Thursday night games.

In recent years, the NFL has begun adding even more games to streaming services. In 2024, Netflix began streaming NFL games on Christmas. Some playoff games are now exclusive to Peacock or Prime Video. The league also has a package called NFL Sunday Ticket, which allows fans to watch any game that doesn't air nationally. Each streaming service has its own price tag. In 2024, it cost $850 for an NFL fan to have access to every game during a season. This is high compared to other leagues.

Regional Battles

The rising cost of broadcasting rights has been a win for most professional leagues and players. Typically leagues agree to share a certain percentage of their revenue with players. As a result, when a league makes more money, the players do too.

RSNs provide teams with another source of money. Like other leagues, MLB shares its national TV money evenly among its 30 teams. But teams don't share the money they make from their RSNs. How much each team makes from their RSN varies greatly. In 2014, the Los Angeles Dodgers signed an RSN deal that pays the team $334 million per year for 25 years. But the Miami Marlins made just $50 million in 2024 from their RSN.

The Los Angeles Dodgers own half the team's RSN, SportsNet LA.

MLB doesn't have a hard salary cap. So the Dodgers can use that extra money to sign better, more expensive players than other teams.

For decades, cable providers paid high prices for RSNs. Streaming's rise in popularity has threatened the existence of many of those channels. With more people leaving behind their cable packages, many RSNs have struggled to stay in business. Some that have stayed in business aren't able to reach deals with cable providers. That has led to many fans not being able to watch their favorite local teams.

A few teams have decided to provide fans with new streaming options. In 2025, MLB.TV began broadcasting local games for five different teams. For $100 a season, fans could watch all their favorite team's games that weren't broadcast nationally. While that price is much cheaper than a cable package, it doesn't include the other local teams in an area. So a Minnesota Twins fan would need another way to watch the Lynx, the Timberwolves, and the Wild.

Throughout history, sports broadcasting has been constantly changing. That continues today. Fans now have more ways to watch sports than ever before. At the same time, the rise in streaming services has made sports TV more complicated and sometimes more expensive. No one is certain where sports broadcasting will go next. But as long as there are sports, people will no doubt be watching them on TV.

Watching sports continues to be one of the United States' favorite pastimes.

PHILA

TIMELINE

1936

The Berlin Olympics becomes the first Olympic Games to be broadcast live.

1950

Nielsen begins recording TV ratings.

1960

The Rome Olympics are the first to be aired internationally on TV.

1970

ABC airs the first NFL *Monday Night Football* game.

1993

FOX buys NFL broadcasting rights and changes how games are presented.

2002

On August 26, MLB becomes the first professional sports league to live stream a regular-season game.

2006

ESPN buys the broadcasting rights for *Monday Night Football.*

2011

FOX begins broadcasting Premier League games in the United States.

2018

ESPN+ launches as a standalone streaming service, offering programming not available on ESPN's TV channels.

2023

MLS sells its broadcasting rights to Apple TV+, becoming the first professional American league to sell its rights to a streaming service.

2024

The streaming service Peacock broadcasts every event from the Olympics to the United States.

2025

CBS airs the Masters for the 70th consecutive year.

GLOSSARY

analyst

In a broadcast, a person who provides details or explanations specific to the topic.

conference

A group of schools that join together to create a league for their sports teams.

contract

A financial agreement.

demographic

A specific characteristic or trait, often used to identify a market.

icon

Someone who is well known.

live stream

To broadcast something online.

on demand

The ability to watch something after it has aired.

pandemic

A widespread outbreak of a disease that affects a large portion of the population.

prime time

The peak time each night when TV ratings are the highest.

regional

Relating to a certain area.

revenue

The amount of money a company makes.

rookie

A professional athlete in their first year of competition.

salary cap

A limit on the amount of money that teams can pay players.

MORE INFORMATION

BOOKS

Dyer, Kristian R. *ESPN: Top Sports News Channel*. Abdo, 2024.

Illustrated Sports Encyclopedia. DK, 2023.

Stathes, Corbu. *Everything Football*. Abdo, 2024.

ONLINE RESOURCES

To learn more about broadcast rights, please visit **abdobooklinks.com** or scan this QR code. These links are routinely monitored and updated to provide the most current information available.

INDEX

ABOUT THE AUTHOR

Luke Hanlon is a sportswriter and editor who lives in Minneapolis, Minnesota. He's written dozens of nonfiction sports books for kids and spends a lot of his free time watching his favorite Minnesota sports teams.